BACK AT ONE
GOD
With

DUANE PHILLIP CAREY JR

To order additional copies of this book, contact:
Xlibris
844-714-8691
www.Xlibris.com
Orders@Xlibris.com

ISBN: Softcover   978-1-6698-2037-6
         EBook   978-1-6698-2038-3

Print information available on the last page

Rev. date: 04/11/2022

Living in this world where there are struggles on every side. Crime plays a big part within our lives where there are home invasions, carjacking, drive-by shootings, store looting, and other adversities that neglect life experiences. We have lost our focus on doing what's right, and maintaining our structure on living righteously. We are stuck with the mindset of doing our own thing, and caring for our own lives.

We have to come back together where everyone can stand on one accord. We were created in the likeness, and image of Christ. God sent his only begotten Son Jesus into the world to die for our sins, and the sins of the entire world. Jesus love for us was so dedicated, and empowered with everlasting life to sustain our lives forevermore. We have to maintain our lives according to the word of God.

Can you imagine the world that we live in given by God maintaining the enlightenment of life? How would life be if everyone stood on one accord in Christ, and understood the importance of standing as one? There would be more advances concerning life experiences, and there wouldn't be any confusion. Think about it if the Devil had not turned against God sin wouldn't have any play. Sin is anything that does not glorify God. If we had a complete understanding of the impact of sin, and how it neglects the abundance of life would we participate our lives within sinning? No, we would apply our understanding, and acknowledgements within the likeness, and image of Christ.

Until we come together to overpower the advances of sin, we would always fall into temptation. Life is a mission given by God to sustain, and impact the living. Without God on our side we find ourselves participating with the advances of sin. Once we are enlightened with the knowledge, and accept God's word as truth. We would have the mindset of living the abundant life that's been given. Can you imagine the impact, and love that we would have to offer one another if we stood on one accord in Christ. Everyone would love one another, help one another, and provide assistance needed to enhance our living. Until we come together as a united nation with the word from our Lord, and Saviour we would walk in the same path that we are accustomed to. Today can be the greatest day of your life once you make the decision to give your life to our Lord, and Savior.

This time, and moment is very exciting for me, because finally we have the opportunity to stand as one. Words can't express the enlightenment, and gratitude of being chosen by God to maintain righteous living. God is good, God is great, we are more than a conqueror to those who love God. Jesus is our only hope of survival as we petition to seek God, our courage, and strength within motivates our living. Life is what we have peace, love, joy, and happiness is what we pray for. Once we come together as one the elements of survival would line up. What motivated my desire was devoting my heart set on living for God. I had to understand that from my past, present, and future life experience. He was there to provide his best for his children. While we continue to advance in life, make no mistake about it, tomorrow isn't promised to any of us. What we have is our right here, and right now at this present time. Anything can happen at any given time. Wouldn't you

feel comfortable knowing that if anything was to happen that would cause you to lose your life your relationship with Christ was at one.

Walk with me as one in Christ Pro 3:5-6 Trust in the Lord with all thine heart, and lean not to your own understanding in all your ways acknowledge him, and He shall direct thy paths. Without God on our side, nothing is possible. We just find ourselves living in a world without direction, perfection, meditation, and Godly reflections that enhance our lives. It's only right that we come to the conclusion of understanding who we are, and acknowledge that we were created to live Holy. Once we have the mindset of seeking our Heavenly Father first then everything else will be added. Make no mistake about it in life I'm sure that you recall living a certain way, and doing certain things that were totally against God. Once you've acknowledge, and accepted salvation from God your mindset was made pure with the divine perfection of faithfulness unto Christ. Now that we are at peace within ourselves, and acknowledge having an enhanced mindset with the enlightenment of Christ.

We are led to live Holy without any misunderstanding of who we are, and who we were created to become. Life is beautiful help us Father without you Lord we can't do anything on our own. But because you came so came so that we would have life, and that more abundantly. We are grateful to acknowledge, and accept your everlasting love within our hearts, and minds. Take control Lord only You know what's best to elevate our hearts, and deliver us from all stress. I thank, and praise you Lord because life without You Lord it's impossible to succeed. Keep living, don't give up, Jesus will supply all your needs. I pray that throughout my expression of words would enlighten, and enhance our understanding to accept what's been given. Trust God with all your heart, mind, and soul, and keep living. We were created to reflect God's image throughout living Holy.

Holiness is moral purity to be set apart, and sanctified for service to God. Once we truly accept who we are, and were created to become nothing can separate us for living for God. A person acts, and speaks from the heart the heart is the center of one's existence. The mind is a reasoning faculty of human beings. Those who reject God have corrupt mindsets. Rom 1: 28 And even as they did not like to retain God in there knowledge, God gave them over to a reprobate mind to do those things which are not convenient; Our soul is part of man's nature which is the seat of our appetites, passions, and emotions. Rom 13:1 Let every soul be subject to the higher powers. For there is no power, but of God: the powers that be are ordained of God.

The body of Christ is a symbolic expression for the church. The risen Christ dwells in His body, and presides over the church. Eph 1:19-23 And what is exceedingly greatness of his power to usward who believe according to the working of mighty power, 20 Which he wrought in Christ when he raised him from the dead, and set him at his right hand in the heavenly places. 21. Far above all principality, and power, and might, and dominion, and every name that is named, not only in this world, but also that which is to come. Our desire of living is totality based on the decisions we make in life. There are only two choices

between right, and wrong. We can choose to follow God which leads unto righteous living. We have the ability to follow the path of unrighteous living that leads to destruction. Which one do you think is best? The choice is yours remember God is in control if there's anything that we desire in life let God order our steps.

He knows what's best, and will supply all that we may think or ask. Honor God's Word, and live for his glory without God we can do nothing. Throughout living according to his instruction we are more than a conqueror to those who love our Lord, and Savior. Give your heart, and mind to our Lord who gave his all so that we can be made whole. Keep living, and remember to always put God first place in life. Because only He can give you an open heart, and mind to remain strong. God is good his mercy, and grace endure within our lives forevermore. Take this this time, and the opportunity to evaluate your life God's way is the best decision you can ever make in life. The choice is yours with God's all things are possible unto those that believe. Make that decision to live your life right.

Wisdom

1. Why is it important to build your house upon the Lord with wisdom? Pro 9:1 Wisdom hath builted her house, she kewn out her seven pillars:

   The seven pillars according to the scriptures are the fear of the Lord, instruction, understanding, discretion, counsel, and reproof.

2. Why is it important to fear the Lord? Pro 9:10 The fear of the Lord is the beginning of wisdom, and the knowledge of the Holy is understanding.

3. Why is it important to speak with wisdom in your heart? Pro 10:13 (In the lips of him that hath understanding wisdom is found, but a rod is for the of him that is void of understanding.

4. Why is it important to know what you say has a cause, and effect? Pro 10:21 The lips of the righteous feed many, but fools die for wisdom.

5. Why does a sinner die without thought? Pro 10:23 It is a sport to a fool to do mischief, but a man of understanding hath wisdom.

6. Why is it important to speak righteously? Pro 10:31 The mouth of the just bringeth forth wisdom, but a forward mouth shall be cut out.

7. Why is it important not to let pride overtake thee? Pro 11:2 (When pride cometh shame, but lowely is wisdom.

8. Why is it important to maintain a mindset of Christ? Pro 11:12 (He that is void of wisdom despiseth his neighbor, but a man of understanding holdeth his peace.

9. Why is it important to guard yourself in the word of God? Pro 11:14 Where the counsel is the people fall; but in the multitude of counselors there is safety.

10. Why is it important to follow God? Pro 10:24 The fear of the wicked it shall come upon him, but the desire of the righteous shall be granted.

11. Why is it important to remain connected to God's word? Pro 13:13 Who despiseth the word shall destroyed, but he that feareth commandment shall be rewarded,

12. Why is it important to abide by God's laws? Pro 13:14 The law of the wise is the fountain of life to depart from the snares of death.

13. Why is it important not to walk with ungodly people? Pro 13:20 (He that walk with wise men, shall be wise, but the companion of fools shall be destroyed.

14. What happens once your understanding is not clear on God, but your mindset seeketh to maintain an understanding? Pro 14:6 A scorner seeketh wisdom, and findeth it not, but knowledge is easy unto him that understandeth.

15. Why is it important to acknowledge your formal way of thinking? Pro 14:8 (The wisdom of the prudent is to understand his way, but the folly of fools is deceit.

16. Why is it important to have a structure of living righteously unto the Lord? Pro 14:25 (A true witness delivered souls, but a deceitful witness speaketh lies.

17. Why is it important to seek God for wisdom? Pro 14:33 Wisdom rested in the heart of him that hath understanding: but that which is in the midst of fools is made known.

18. Why is it normal for us to live according to the way we have been living? Pro 15:21 (Folly is to him that is destitute of wisdom, but a man of understanding walks uprightly.

19. Why is it important to know wisdom, and instruction? Pro 1:1 To know wisdom, and instruction is to perceive the words of understanding.

20. Why is it important to receive instruction from God? Pro 1:2 To receive the instruction of wisdom, justice, judgment, and equity.

21. Why is it important to live by the word of truth? Pro 1:23 Turn at my reproof; behold I will pour out my Spirit unto you, I will make known my words unto you.

22. What happens once you commit to the Lord? Pro 2:1 My son, if thou wilt receive my words, and hide my commandment with thee.

23. Why is it important to say what God say? Pro 2:6 For the Lord giveth wisdom, and out of his mouth cometh knowledge, and understanding.

24. Why is it important to walk with the enlightenment of God, and maintain sound doctrine? Pro 2:7 He layeth up sound wisdom for the righteous: He is a buckler to them that walk uprightly.

25. Why is it important to be grounded by wisdom in your heart? Pro 2:10 When wisdom entered in thine heart, and knowledge is pleasant unto thy soul.

26. Why is it important to have a goal, and have a path that leads to success? Pro2:20 That thou mayest walk in the way of good men, and keep the path of the righteous.

27. Why is it important to understand, and receive correction from the Lord? Pro 3:12 For whom the Lord loveth He correcteth; even as a Father the Son in whom He delighteth.

28. Why is it important to understand why wisdom was founded upon the earth? Pro 3:19 The Lord by wisdom hath founded the earth: by understanding hath established the heavens.

29. Why is it important to study God's laws in the bible? Pro 3:21 (My son let not them depart from thine eyes: keep sound wisdom, and discretion.

30. What's the benefit of following God's laws? Pro 3:25 Do not afraid of sudden fear neither of the desolation of the wicked when it cometh.

Counsel: Advice especially that's given formally. With wise counsel a couple can buy a home that will be appreciating in value.

Reproof: A expression of blame or disapproval

Knowledge

1. Why is it important to walk in the ways of the Lord? Pro 8:32 Now therefore hearken unto me, O ye children for blessed are they that keep my ways.

2. Why is it important to acknowledge God's presence everyday? Pro 118:24 This is the day that the Lord has made, we will rejoice, and be glad in it.

3. 3 Why is it important to fear God first in your heart? Pro 1:7 The fear of the Lord is the beginning of knowledge, but fools despise wisdom, and instruction.

4. Why is it important not to be followers of the wicked? Ps 27:2 When the wicked even mine enemies, and my foes came upon me to eat my flesh they stumbled, and fell.

5. Why is it important to commit all your ways unto the Lord? Ps 37:5 Commit thy way unto the Lord: trust also in him, and he shall bring it to pass.

6. Why is it important to hear God's instruction? John 8:47 He that is of God heareth God's words, ye therefore hear them not because ye are not of God.

7. Why is it important to keep your mind on Jesus? Isa 26:3 Thou will keep him in perfect peace whose mind is stayed on thee, because he trusted in thee.

8. Why is it important to trust God for understanding? Phil 4:7 And the peace of God which passeth all understanding, and shall keep your hearts through Christ Jesus.

9. What are the benefits of receiving salvation from God? Eze 36:26 A new heart will I give you, and a new Spirit will I put within you, and take away the stony heart out of your flesh, and I will give you a new heart of flesh.

10. Why is it important to acknowledge being chosen to walk according to the Spirit of God? Eze 36:27 And I will put my Spirit within you, and cause you to walk in my statutes, and ye shall keep my judgements, and do them.

11. Why is it important to believe that living for God is right? Gen 15: 6 (And he believed in the Lord, and he counted to him for righteousness.

12. Why is it important for children to come together as a united nation for Christ? Isa 1:18 Come now let us reason together saith the Lord though your sins be as scarlet they shall be white as snow, though they be red like crimson they shall be as wool.

13. Why is it important to live with the knowledge of God? Pro 22:12 The eyes of the Lord preserve knowledge, and he overthroweth the mouth of the transgressor.

14. Why is it important to keep your focus on God? Jer 29:13 And ye shall seek me and find me and when ye shall search for me with all your heart.

15. Why is it important to seek knowledge, and have a heart to maintain knowledge? Pro 18:15 The heart of the prudent getteth knowledge, and the ear of the wise seeketh knowledge.

16. Why did God instruct us to show thyself approved in His sight? Pro 22:12 The eyes of the Lord preserve knowledge, and he overthroweth the word of the transgressor.

17. Why is it important to remain strong in the Lord? Pro 24:5 A wise man is strong yea a man of knowledge increaseth knowledge.

18. Why is it important to seek God's scripture for wisdom, and instruction? 2 Tim 3:16 All scripture is given by inspiration of God, and is profitable for doctrine, for reproof, for correction, for instruction in righteousness.

19. Why is it important to seek after wisdom, and knowledge unto the Lord? Pro 3:20 By His knowledge the depths are broken up, and the clouds drop down the dew.

20. Why is it important to have a sincere heart to seek God? Pro 2:3 Yea if thou criest after knowledge, and liftest up thy voice for understanding.

21. Why is it important to maintain control over how you speak? Pro 8:8 All the words of my mouth are in righteousness there is nothing froward or perverse in them.

22. Why is it important to understand the acknowledgement of God? Pro 8:9 They are all plain to them that understandeth, and right to them that findeth knowledge.

23. Why is it important to speak the truth in all your ways? Pro 8:7 For my mouth shall speak truth, a wickedness is an abomination to my lips.

24. Why is it important to hearken unto the Lord, and keep his ways? Pro 8:32 Now therefore hearken unto me, ye children for blessed are they that keep my ways.

25. What are the benefits for desiring to have a sincere search for God? Pro 8:35 For whoso findeth me findeth life and shall obtain favor from the Lord.

26. Why is it important to know your position as a man of God? Pro 22:20 Have I not written to thee excellent things in castle, and knowledge.

27. Why is it important to speak with the knowledge of God? Pro 2:6 For the Lord give its wisdom out of his mouth commeth knowledge and understanding.

28. Why is it important to use your freedom of speech wisely? Pro 15:7 The lips of the wise disperse knowledge, but the heart of the foolish doesn't not so.

Understanding

1. Why is it important to maintain a clear understanding in the Lord? Pro 1:5 A wise man will hear, and will increase learning: and a man of understanding shall attain unto wise counsels.

2. What happens once you make the decision to follow Jesus? Pro 15 14 The heart of him that hath understanding seeketh knowledge, but the mouth of fools feedeth on foolishness.

3. What are the benefits of accepting Jesus as your Lord, and Savior? Eph 1:17 That the God of our Lord Jesus Christ, the Father of Glory may give unto you the Spirit of wisdom, and revelation in the knowledge of him.

4. Why is it important to know that God will guide you in the way that you should go in life? Eph 1:18 The eyes of your understanding being enlightened that ye may know what is the hope of His calling, and what the riches of the glory of his inheritance in the saints.

5. Why is it important to apply your speech level positively? Pro 10:13 (In the lips of him that hath understanding wisdom is found: but a rod is for the back of him that is void of understanding.

6. Why is it important to trust God's way of living instead of embracing the world's way of living? Rom 12:2 And be not conformed to this world: but be ye transformed by the renewing of your mind that ye may prove what is that good, and acceptable, and perfect will of God.

7. Why is it important to study the word of God? Pro 15:28 (The heart of the righteous studieth to answer, but the mouth of the wicked poureth out evil things.

8. What happens once you make the decision not to walk according to the word of God? Pro 15:32 He that refuseth instruction despiseth his own soul, but he that heareth reproof getteth understanding.

9. What is the reward for walking according to the knowledge of God? Pro 14:18 (The simple inherit folly: but the prudent inherit folly; but the prudent are crowned with knowledge.

10. What's the advantage of being rooted, and instructed by God? 1Jn 3:9 Whosoever is born of God doth not sin: for his seed remaineth in him; and he cannot sin because he is born of God.

11. What is the message from God that we heard from the beginning that we should abide by? 1 Jn 3:11 (For this is the message that ye have heard from the beginning that we should love one another.

Communication

1. Why is it important to speak with the knowledge of God in your heart? Job 33:3 My words shall be the uprighteous of my heart, and my lips shall utter knowledge clearly.

2. Why is it important to hear the word of God? Job 34:2 Hear my words, O ye wise men, and give ear unto me ye that have knowledge.

3. Why is it important to acknowledge God's word as truth? Job 36:4 For truly my words shall not be false He that is perfect in knowledge is with thee.

4. Why is it important to maintain your speech accordingly throughout living for God? Pro 15:14 The heart of him that had understanding seek his knowledge, but the mouth of the fools feedeth on foolishness.

5. Why is it important to trust God for wisdom? Pro 2:6 The Lord giveth wisdom out of his mouth cometh knowledge, and understanding.

6. Why is it important to speak positively? Pro 15:2 The tongue of the wise useth knowledge alright, but the mouth of the fools poureth out foolishness.

7. How can you tell when a person is truly devoted to the acknowledgement of God? Pro 17:27 He that hath knowledge speareth his words, and a man of understanding is of an excellent spirit.

8. Why is it important to maintain God instruction of speech while facing temptation? Ps 39:1 I said I will take heed to my ways that I sin not with my tongue I will keep my mouth with a bridle while the wicked is before me.

9. Why is it important to understand your freedom of speech? Pro 10:11 The mouth of a righteous man is a well of life, but violence covereth the mouth of the wicked.

10. Why is it important to acknowledge the difference between positive language, and improper language? Pro 13:3 He that keepeth his mouth, keeprth his life, but violence covereth the mouth of the wicked.

Instruction

1. Why is it important to take God's instructions to heart? Pro 15:32 He that refuseth instruction despiseth his own soul, but he that heareth reproof getteth understanding.

2. Why is it important to be wise, and receive instruction? Pro21:11 When the scorner is punished the simple is made wise, and when the wise is instructed he receiveth knowledge.

3. Why is it important to take God's instruction to apply knowledge? Pro 23:12 Apply thy heart unto instruction, and thine ears to the words of knowledge.

4. What happens once you become observant, and open minded to receive God's instruction? Pro24:32 Then I saw, and considered it well: I looked upon it, and received instruction.

5. Why is it important to receive the Lord with the instruction of wisdom? Pro 15:33 The fear of the Lord is the instruction of wisdom, and before honor is humility.

6. Why is it important to receive counsel, and instruction? Pro 19:20 Hear counsel, and receive instruction that thou mayest be wise in thy latter end.

7. What happens once you make the decision between right, and wrong? Pro 19:27 Cease my son to hear my instruction that causeth to err from the words of knowledge.

8. What happens once we make the decision to hear God's word? Pro 4:1 Hear ye children the instruction of a father, and attend to know understanding.

9. Why is it important to take God's Commandments as law? Pro 6:23 For the commandment is a lamp, and the law is light; and reproofs of instruction are the way of life.

10. Why is it important to hear God's instruction? Pro 1:7 The fear of the Lord is the beginning of knowledge, but fools despise wisdom, and instruction.

11. What are the four elements of receiving God's instruction? Pro 1:3 To receive the instruction of wisdom, justice, judgement, and equity.

12. Why is it important to be a wise son unto God: Pro 13:1 A wise son heareth his father's instruction, but a scorner heareth not rebuke.

13. Why is it important to consider God's instruction? Pro 8:33 Hear instructure, and be wise, and refuse it not.

14. Why is it important to accept the truth to maintain a proper understanding? Pro 23:23 Buy the truth, and sell it not also wisdom, instruction, and understanding.

15. What happens once you make the choice to walk according to God's instruction? Pro 5:23 He shall die without instruction, and in the greatness of his folly he shall go astray.

Holy

1. Eph 4:24 And that ye put on the new man, which after God is created in righteousness, and true holiness.

2. Mt 5:48 (Be ye therefore perfect, even as your Father which is in heaven is perfect.

3. Rom 15:33 Now the God of hope fill you with all joy, and peace in believing that ye may abound in hope through the power of the Holy Ghost.

4. Pro 18:4 (The words of a man's mouth are as deep waters, and the wellspring of wisdom as a flowing brook.

5. Ps 37:4 Delight thyself in the Lord, and He shall give thee the desires of your heart.

6. 1 Cor 2:16 (For who hath the He may instruct him? But we have the mind of Christ.

7. Job 42:2 I know thou canst do everything, and that no thought can be withholden from thee.

Sanctified

1. 1 Cor 6:11 And such were some of you: but ye are washed, but ye are sanctified, but ye are justified in the name of the Lord Jesus, and by the Spirit of our God.

2. 1 Pet 3:15 But sanctify the Lord in your hearts, and be ready always to give an answer to every man that asketh you a reason of the hope that is in you with meekness, and fear.

3. Acts 4:12 Neither is there salvation in any other other, for there is none other name under heaven given among men, whereby we must be saved.

4. 1 Jn 3:10 In this the children of God are manifest, and the children of the Devil: whoever doth not righteousness is not of God, neither he that loveth not his brother.

5. Pro 18:1 Through desire a man having seperated himself, seeketh and intermeddleth with all wisdom. 2 A fool hath no delight in understanding, but that his heart may discover itself.

Faith

1. What was Jesus' response for our needs being met through faith, and prayer? Mt 21:21-22 Jesus answered, and said unto them, verily I say unto you, If ye have faith, and doubt not, ye shall not only do this which is done to the fig tree, but also if ye shall say unto this mountain, be ye removed, and be thou cast unto the sea; it shall be done. 22 And all things, whatsoever ye shall ask in prayer, believing ye shall receive.

2. Why is it important to have faith within our prayer request to God? Heb 11:1 Now faith is the substance of things hoped for, the evidence of things not seen.

3. Why is it important to have faith in God believing that all your needs will be met? Mt 11:24 Therefore I say unto you, what things soever ye desire when ye pray, believe that ye receive them, and ye shall have them.

4. Why is it important to live, and walk by faith according to scripture? Jn 7:38 He that believeth on me as the scripture has said out of his belly shall flow rivers of water.

5. Why is it important to have faith, even a grain of mustard seed? Mt 17:20 And Jesus said unto them: because of your unbelief, for verily I say unto you, if ye have faith as a grain of mustard seed, ye shall say to this mountain, Remove hence to yonder place, and it shall be removed: and nothing shall be impossible unto you.

6. Why is it important to have faith in God, and doubt not? Mt 21:21 Jesus answered, and said, and said unto them, Verily I say unto you, if ye have faith, and doubt not, ye shall not only do this which is done to the fig tree, but also ye shall say unto the mountain; be thou removed, and be thou cast into the sea: it shall be done.

7. What happens once you make the decision to do your own thing after receiving instruction from God? Jn 8:24 I said therefore unto you, thay ye shall die in your sins.

8. Why is it important to be strengthen with might by faith in God within your heart: Eph 3:16-17 That He would grant you, according to the riches of his glory to be strengthened with might by his Spirit in the inner man.

9. Why is it important to have an ear to receive God's instruction while walking by faith? Rom 10:17 So then faith cometh by hearing, and hearing by the word of God.

10. Why is it important to understand the benefits of accepting salvation? Eph 2:8-9 For by grace ye are saved through faith, and that not of yourselves, it is the gift of God: 9 Not of works lest any man should boast.

11. Why is it important to have faith in God to fill you with all power? Rom 15:13 Now the God of hope fills you with all joy, and peace in believing that ye may abound in hope, through the power of the Holy Ghost.

12. Why is it important to have faith while thrusting God? Pro3:5-6 Trust in the lord with all thine heart, and lean not unto thine own understanding. 6 In all thy way acknowledge him, and He shall direct thy paths.

13. Why is it important to have faith in the word of God? Jn 6:35 And Jesus said unto them, I am the bread of life; he that cometh to me shall never hunger; and he that believeth on me shall never thirst.

14. Why is it important to understand, and recognize the power of God? Jn 1:12 He came unto his own, But as many as received him, to them He gave power to become the sons of God even to them that believe on his name.

15. Why is it important to walk according to the faith of God? Jam 1:6 But let him ask in faith, nothing wavering. For he that wavereth is like a wave of the sea driven with the wind, and tossed.

Instruction of Speech

1. All The Words Of My Mouth: Pro 8:8 All the words of my mouth are in righteousness there is nothing froward or perverse in them.

2. Blessings Are Upon The Head Of The Just: Pro 10 6 Blessings are upon the head of the just, but violence covereth the mouth of the wicked.

3. The Tongue Of The Just: Pro 10:20 The tongue of the just is as choice silver, but the heart of the wicked is little worth.

4. The Lips Of The Righteous: Pro 10:21 The lips of the righteous feed many: but fools die for want of wisdom.

5. The Mouth Of The Just: Pro 10:31 The mouth of the just bringeth forth wisdom, but the froward tongue shall be cut out.

6. The Lips Of The Righteous: Pro 10:32 The lips of the righteous knows what is acceptable, but the mouth of the wicked poureth out foolishness.

7. A Man Shall Be Satisfied By The Fruit O His Mouth: Pro 12:14 A man shall be satisfied with good by the fruit of his mouth, and the recompense of a man's hands shall be rendered unto him.

8. Speak Truth To Live Righteously unto God: Pro 12:17 He that speaketh truth sheweth forth righteousness, but a false witness deceit.

9. The Lips Of The Truth Shall Be Established Forever: Pro 12:19 The lip of truth shall be established forever; but a lying tongue is but for a moment.

10. A Wise Man Heareth His Father's Instruction: Pro 13:1 A wise son heareth his Father's instruction, but a scorner heareth not rebuke.

11. Scorner: A person who express contempt or disdain for someone or something.

12. A Man Shall Eat Good By The Fruit Of His Mouth: Pro 13:2 A man shall eat good by the fruit of his mouth: but a scorner heareth not rebuke.

13. He That Keepeth His Mouth Keepeth His Life: Pro 13:3 The soul that keepeth his mouth keepeth his life, but he that open wide his lips shall have destruction.

14. Flattering lips: Ex 6:12 And Moses spake before the Lord saying, Behold the children of Israel have not hearkened unto me; how then shall Pharaohthe children hear me who am of uncircumcised lips.

15. Putting Instruction In Writting: Deut 31:9 (And Moses wrote this law, and delivered unto the priest the sons of Levi which bare the ark of the Lord, and unto all the elders of Israel.

16. Communication With The Dead: 1Sam 28:8 And Saul disguised himself, and put on other raiment, and he went, and two men by night with him, and they came to the woman, and he said, I pray thee divine unto me by the familiar spirit, and bring me him up whom I shall name unto thee.

17. Communication Methods: 2 Chro 30:8 Now be ye not stiffnecked as your father's were, but yeild yourselves unto the Lord, and enter into his sanctuary which He hath sanctified for ever, and serve the Lord your God that the fierceness of his wrath may turn away from you.

18. Left With Nothing To Say: Neh 5:8 And I said unto them, we after our ability have redeemed our brethren the Jews the Jews were sold unto the heathen? and will ye even sell your brethren? or shall they be sold unto us? Then held they their peace, and found nothing to answer.

19. Windy Conversation: Job 8:2 How long wilt thou speak these things? and how long shall the words of thy mouth be like a strong wind.

20. Resolving Not To Sin With Thou Mouth: Ps 17:3 Hold up my goings in thy paths that my foot steps slip not. 3 Thou hast proved mine heart: thou hast visited me in the night, thou hast tried me, and shall find nothing: I am purposed that my mouth shall not transgress.

21. Serpent Tongue: Ps 140:3 Set a watch, O Lord before my mouth: keep the door of my lips.

22. Words Known Before Spoken: Ps 139:4 For there is not a word in my tongue, but lo O Lord thou knowest it altogether.

23. Keeping Tongue: Ps 39:1 I said I will take heed to my ways that I sin not with my tongue; i will keep my mouth with a bridle while the wicked is before me.

24. How To Avoid Gossip: Ps 141:3 Set a watch, O Lord before my mouth, keep the door of my lips.

25. Speech Of Righteousness: Pro 10:11 (The mouth of a righteous man is a well of life, but violence covereth the mouth of the wicked.

26. Instructed Tongue: Isa 50:4 The Lord hath given me the tongue of the learned that should know how to speak a word in season to him that is weary: He wakeneth morning by morning, He wakeneth mine ear to hear as the learned.

27. Communicating With God: Ps 18:25 With the merciful thou wilt show thyself merciful with an upright man thou shew thyself upright.

28. Boldness Of Speech Given By God: Jer 1:6 Then said I, Ah, Lord God; behold I cannot speak for I am a child.

29. Good News Between Believers: Phil 2:19 But I trust in the Lord Jesus to send Timothues shortly unto you, that I also may be of good comfort, when I know your state.

30. Communication With Followers: Col 4:8 Whom I have sent unto you for the same purpose that he might know your estate, and comfort your hearts.

31. Good, And Evil Tongue: Pro 10:31 32 The mouth of the just bringeth forth wisdom, but the forward shall be cut out. 32 The lips of the righteous know what is acceptable, but the mouth of the wicked speaketh frowardness.

32. Follish Talk: Eph 5:4 Neither filthiness, nor foolish talking, nor jesting.

33. Guard Tongue Well:Jam 3:5-6 Even so the tongue is a little member, and boasteth great things. Behold how great a matter a little fire kindleth! 6 And the tongue is afire, a world of iniquity: so is the tongue among our members, that is defileth the whole body, and setteth on fire the course of nature; and it is set on fire of hell.

34. Be Not Rashed With Thy Mouth: Ecc 5:2 Be not rashed with thy mouth, and let not thine heart be hasty to utter anything before God; for God is in heaven, and thou upon earth let thy words be few.

35. To Be Free From The Tongue Of Evil: Pro 6:24 keep thee from the evil woman from the flattery of the tongue of the strange woman.

36. Every Word That's Spoken Shall Give Account: Mt 12:36 But I say unto you, That every idle word that men shall speak they shall give account thereof in the day of judgement.

Printed in the United States
by Baker & Taylor Publisher Services